GRIZZLIES

by Lynn M. Stone

A Carolrhoda Nature Watch Book

 Carolrhoda Books, Inc./Minneapolis

In memory of Jason—best friend, brother, and bear-country companion, who left us much too soon

Carolrhoda Books, Inc., c/o The Lerner Group
241 First Avenue North, Minneapolis, Minnesota 55401

LIBRARY OF CONGRESS CATALOGING-IN-PUBLICATION DATA

Stone, Lynn M.
    Grizzlies / by Lynn M. Stone
        p.   cm.
    "A Carolrhoda nature watch book."
    Includes index.
    Summary: Describes the physical characteristics, behavior, and habitat of brown bears in general and grizzly bears in particular, and discusses differences between them and other bear species.
    ISBN 0-87614-800-3
    1. Grizzly bear—Juvenile literature. 2. Grizzly bear— Alaska—McNeil River State Game Sanctuary—Juvenile literature. 3. Brown bear—Juvenile literature. 4. Brown bear—Alaska—McNeil River State Game Sanctuary— Juvenile literature. [1. Grizzly bear. 2. Brown bear. 3. Bears.] I. Title.
    QL737.C27S77 1993
    599.74'446—dc20   93-22074
                                              CIP
                                               AC

Manufactured in the United States of America

2 3 4 5 6 – P/JR – 98 97 96 95

🐻 NOTE TO READERS 🐻

Grizzlies are magnificent animals that can be dangerous. Therefore, always treat them with respect and caution. NEVER approach a bear of any kind in the wild. Stay as far away from them as possible. For safety tips on traveling in bear country, talk to a park ranger in the area or write to:

Center for Wildlife Information
P.O. Box 885
Bloomfield Hills, MI 48303

The author wishes to thank the following for their help in the preparation of this book: Dr. Charles Jonkel; Derek Stonorov, Larry Aumiller, John Trent, and the Alaska Department of Fish and Game; Vivian Banci and the Wildlife Branch of the British Columbia Ministry of Environment, Lands, and Parks.

Each summer, on a windy Alaskan peninsula southwest of Anchorage, the McNeil River becomes the home of the local giants club. The local giants are big brown bears. Fifty, sixty, or more of them gather at the falls, where the river narrows and pitches downward in cascades and swirling pools.

From June to August, salmon from the Pacific Ocean swim upstream into the McNeil. This is the river in which these fish were born, and now they return to lay their eggs. As they surge upriver, the salmon bottle up in pools below the swift, rocky falls and become tasty **prey** for the bears.

Nowhere else on earth do so many brown bears gather together. And nowhere else can people watch so many wild grizzlies at such close range. Human visitors to the McNeil River State Game Sanctuary watch the fishing bears from a slope just a few steps from the river. No fences or walls separate the four-legged animals from the two-legged.

7

In the 1800s and early 1900s, grizzlies were portrayed in American stories and advertising as ferocious, malicious beasts. A famous mountain man of the American West, Jim Bridger, called grizzlies "devils in fur coats."

These planned close encounters between people and grizzly bears are something quite new. Until recently, the brown bear was regarded as a highly dangerous beast, best turned into a rug. But as scientists have had a chance to study wild brown bears and people have learned about them, we have come to see far more than just danger in these animals.

8

The grizzly, or brown bear, is one of eight **species,** or kinds, of bears found in the world. Two other species are well known in North America—the polar bear and the American black bear. As for the remaining species, the sun bear, the sloth bear, the Asian black bear, and the giant panda live in Asia, and the spectacled bear lives in South America.

A polar bear (above), *a spectacled bear* (right), *and an American black bear* (below)

A European brown bear

Scientists used to think there were many kinds of brown bears. It seemed unlikely that the different brown bears of such places as Alaska, California, and Iran could all belong to the same species. For example, brown bears from some parts of Alaska weigh up to six times more than the smallest brown bears elsewhere.

However, after studying bear blood, skull shapes, and skeletons, scientists have lumped all the world's brown bears—European, Asian, and North American—into one species, *Ursus arctos*. The scientists decided the size differences between the bears are mostly due to the differences in what the bears have eaten over the centuries. Brown bears that have fed on salmon have grown much larger than brown bears without this food source.

A Kodiak brown bear (opposite)

To describe some of the most important differences between the brown bears, scientists divided the species into races, or **subspecies**. Bear experts differ on the number of brown bear subspecies in the world. Most scientists agree, however, that all the North American brown bears belong to just two subspecies.

The subspecies *Ursus arctos middendorffi* describes the brown bears found on Kodiak Island, Alaska, and nearby islands. These islands were separated from the Alaskan mainland by the activity of glaciers about 10,000 years ago. Over the thousands of years since, the island bears ate better than their mainland cousins and became exceptionally large. Known as Kodiak brown bears, they may exceed 1,500 pounds (675 kg).

As far as science is concerned, all the rest of the brown bears in North America are *Ursus arctos horribilis,* or grizzly bears. The name grizzly comes from the fact that the North American brown bear has long fur that often has silver or whitish tips, giving the bear a gray-haired or "grizzled" look.

The term grizzly, though, can be confusing. Some people in the Northwest make a distinction between grizzlies and what they call "brownies," or Alaskan brown bears. For them, brownies are the coastal brown bears of British Columbia and Alaska, which gorge on salmon and grow very large. "Grizzlies" are the brown bears that live at least 75 miles (120 km) from a sea coast and are generally a little smaller.

In this book, we will use grizzly to mean any North American brown bear that is not a Kodiak.

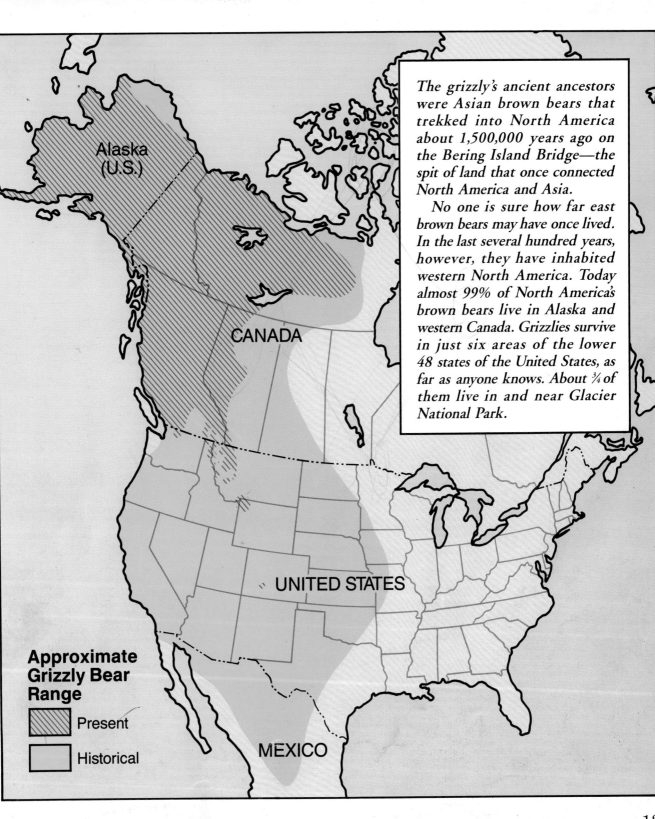

The grizzly's ancient ancestors were Asian brown bears that trekked into North America about 1,500,000 years ago on the Bering Island Bridge—the spit of land that once connected North America and Asia.

No one is sure how far east brown bears may have once lived. In the last several hundred years, however, they have inhabited western North America. Today almost 99% of North America's brown bears live in Alaska and western Canada. Grizzlies survive in just six areas of the lower 48 states of the United States, as far as anyone knows. About ¾ of them live in and near Glacier National Park.

Alaska (U.S.)

CANADA

UNITED STATES

MEXICO

Approximate Grizzly Bear Range

Present

Historical

Whatever one calls them, brown bears of North America are magnificent beasts—huge, powerful, agile, and intelligent. The bears have claws more than 4 inches (10 cm) long and teeth nearly 3 inches (7.5 cm) long. Huge shoulder muscles form a "hump" across their upper backs.

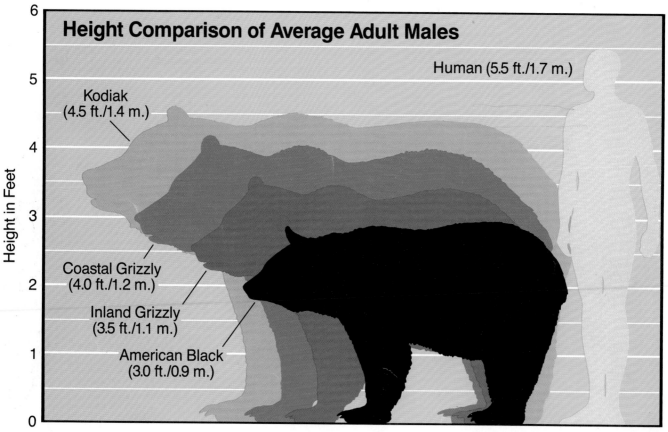

Height Comparison of Average Adult Males

Human (5.5 ft./1.7 m.)

Kodiak (4.5 ft./1.4 m.)

Coastal Grizzly (4.0 ft./1.2 m.)

Inland Grizzly (3.5 ft./1.1 m.)

American Black (3.0 ft./0.9 m.)

Height in Feet

When a large male grizzly stands on its hind feet, its nose is 10 feet (3 m) from the ground. If it stood under a basketball hoop, the bear's head would bump the rim. On the court, it would barrel along at 35 miles (22.5 m) per hour, much faster than a professional basketball player could sprint.

Inland brown bears, those that live more than 75 miles (120 km) from a seacoast, weigh between 150 and 600 pounds (67.5 and 270 kg). Coastal brown bears are much heavier, rivaling the heavyweights of Kodiak Island.

A coastal grizzly

When a brown bear wants to smell something more clearly, it stands up on its back feet. There it can catch a whiff of the smells on the stronger, higher drafts of wind.

Though grizzlies are called brown bears, they have fur of various shades—from quite blond to reddish brown to nearly black. Because of the range of colors of grizzlies, they are sometimes confused with American black bears, or *Ursus americanus.*

Black bears are generally black, but their fur may also be brown, blond, whitish, or even bluish. In Yellowstone National Park, a park shared by black bears and grizzlies, many of the black bears have brown fur. At 150 to 500 pounds (67.5 to 255 kg), black bears are usually smaller than grizzlies. They lack the grizzly "hump," and they have shorter fur and shorter claws, which are more useful for climbing trees.

A cinnamon-colored American black bear

16

Brown bears and black bears share some of the same kinds of surroundings, or **habitats.** Brown bears like fairly open country—mountain meadows, river valleys, coastal beaches, grasslands, and the broad, treeless sweep of arctic lands. Though grizzlies used to be found as far south as Mexico and at least as far east as the Mississippi River, they are now mostly an animal of the West and Northwest. Black bears tend to like more wooded areas than grizzlies, such as forests and swamps near meadow areas. Black bears are found from Alaska to Newfoundland and south to Mexico.

Within its habitat, a grizzly needs to find water, plentiful food, and a safe, comfortable place to den in the winter. Having enough food available is extremely important for such a large animal. A brown bear is an **omnivore**, an animal that eats both plants and other animals. It downs 26 to 35 pounds (11.7 to 15.75 kg) of food on an average day and almost three times that as winter nears. The bulk of its diet is usually from plants—leaves, green shoots, bulbs, wildflowers, grasses, berries, and nuts.

But a brown bear eats whatever it has the opportunity to eat. Long-time naturalist Olaus Murie once observed that almost everything a grizzly found was food "except granite."

Brown bears have a taste for squirrels, and they use their shoulder muscles to turn meadows into moonscapes as they dig up ground squirrel burrows. Nor are these huge bears above raiding a beehive or turning over rocks and logs to find a meal of ants.

A grizzly has the keen senses of a

predator, or hunting animal. It probably has the best sense of smell of any North American animal. It can detect a piece of gum in the glove compartment of a car or cooking smoke on a person's clothes. Brown bears have excellent hearing and eyesight that rivals a person's. They hunt successfully by night and day. The great brown bear has all the physical tools it needs to be a powerful predator too—incredible strength, amazing speed, sharp teeth, and five knifelike claws on each paw.

19

With its massive shoulder muscles, a grizzly can knock an elk off its feet. Even so, a brown bear rarely attacks large, full-grown animals unless they are sick or injured.

Grizzlies prefer to hunt young or newborn animals, such as the calves of elk, deer, or caribou. Adult male grizzlies even attack bear cubs. Most times, however, it's easier to feed on animals that are already dead, or **carrion.** Grizzlies will scavenge what carrion they can find or steal from wolves, coyotes, and other bears.

Grizzlies that live along the Pacific coast, like the McNeil River bears, are particularly fond of salmon. Each seems to use its own fishing method. Many bears trap salmon against the stream bottom with their paws. Others, by snorkeling, belly flopping, or swimming underwater, grab salmon in their jaws.

If grizzlies lived year-round on salmon, it's almost frightening to think how large they might grow. A brown bear can eat up to 90 pounds (40.5 kg) of salmon and gain up to 6 pounds (2.7 kg) of fat in 24 hours. But salmon are not available all year, so the coastal grizzlies enrich their diets with other food.

While fishing for salmon, grizzlies enjoy getting wet. They don't sweat, so they depend on dips like this or panting to cool off. They also shed or rub off their winter coats in midsummer, then start building up a new coat in the fall.

Within brown-bear habitats, each bear has its own neighborhood, or **home range.** The home range is the total area in which one grizzly normally roams. The home range of one bear can overlap the home ranges of others.

Each section of a grizzly's home range has some special attraction to the bear at one time of the year or another. The McNeil River is within the home ranges of about 100 grizzlies. Every summer, it attracts these bears when the salmon return.

The salmon **migrations**—their journeys from ocean to stream—begin in June and continue through October. Each of the five Pacific salmon species is on a different schedule in the various streams. Like a bargain hunter, a grizzly may fish in one stream in June, another in July, and a third in August.

Afterward, the bear moves on, perhaps to a mountain meadow for its ripe berry patch. A brown bear's travels cross-country are usually for one purpose: finding food.

The size of a brown bear's home range varies. Where food is plentiful, grizzlies do not need to travel long distances. In places where food is scarce, there are fewer brown bears and they have larger home ranges.

On Admiralty Island, near Juneau, Alaska, the habitat for brown bears is excellent. Salmon streams and plant-rich mountain meadows are a grizzly's delight. The numerous grizzlies on Admiralty may have home ranges of only 10 square miles (26 sq km). In mountainous northern Alaska, where bear food is not nearly as plentiful, a grizzly may wander a home range of 130 square miles (338 sq km).

Male grizzlies have home ranges two to four times the size of those of females. A larger animal, the male needs more food, and it has more freedom to explore. The female spends most of her adult life shepherding cubs. She cannot move any farther or faster than her cubs.

Brown bears are faithful to their neighborhoods. Sometimes grizzlies are trapped and removed to another area by scientists or wildlife managers. The bear's **homing instinct,** or its ability to find its way back, is remarkable. At least eight grizzlies have returned to their homes after being released more than 125 miles (200 km) away. Scientists are puzzled by the bears' homing ability. The bears' amazingly sharp sense of smell may play a role, as may their intelligence. Grizzlies are known for their curiosity and ability to learn complex ideas and tasks quickly. Many a grizzly has outsmarted the hunter or wildlife manager who has tried to lure it into a trap.

In general, adult grizzlies often share home ranges, or parts of home ranges, with people and other grizzlies, but the bears avoid both, except in unusual circumstances. Bear talk—grunts, growls, and booming roars—helps bears stay aware of each other's presence and intentions. Grizzlies also scrape, chew, and rub trees. The trees may be signposts to let other bears know who is in the neighborhood or whose neighborhood it is.

Adult males travel alone. When grizzlies do gather together at a salmon stream, they act nervous and cranky. The bears watch one another continually. With growls or earthshaking roars, large bears frighten smaller bears away from their "private" pools.

Bears also communicate their anger or discomfort with body language—open mouths, raised snouts, flattened ears, and other gestures. When actions like these fail, a grizzly may charge on all fours. Sometimes it's a bluff, but an aggressive bear may actually attack.

Females are a little more social. Twin mothers sometimes travel together with their cubs, with one babysitting while the other looks for food. Most of the time, however, females keep company only with their cubs. Fishing with other bears is especially tough on a mother with young cubs. The bear must try to catch salmon while making sure her cubs do not stray near the fishing hole of an adult male.

Males and females have no interest in each other except during the brief mating season in June. Then a lone female, or one with two-and-a-half-year-old cubs, invites the attention of a male. (The cubs wisely flee at the male bear's approach.)

The male travels with the female for 10 or 12 days. During that time, the male may leave one female to mate with another. Females also try to mate with more than one male. Fights between courting males sometimes occur, but they are not common. Within two or three weeks, the courtship season is over. Each adult bear returns to its private journey.

Grizzlies spend summer and especially autumn days picnicking. Gaining weight is serious business for brown bears. Without a hefty fat reserve, a grizzly may not survive the winter. So the bear bulks up, and with a layer of fat up to 10 inches (25 cm) thick, it will eventually retire to sleep winter away.

The grizzly chooses a new, clean den in its home range each fall. The new den is often near an old one. The bear may dig a hole on a hillside, take over a natural cave, or dig out a hollow under a tree. A short tunnel usually leads into the sleeping chamber. The bear drags branches and grasses into this room for bedding.

Pregnant females go to their dens first, sometimes as early as October. Males retire later, usually after winter's first heavy snow. Tucked away, the grizzly falls into a deep, prolonged sleep, or **hibernation.** In hibernation, the grizzly's body systems slow down dramatically. Its body temperature drops about 9° from its normal range of 89° to 99°F (32° to 37.5°C), and its heart rate slows from 40 to 50 beats per minute to just 8 beats per minute. It uses only half the oxygen it does when it is active.

The hibernating grizzly does not eat or drink. It lives off its fat. Naturally, the bear loses weight—up to 40 percent of its total weight—but not enough to be a threat to its life.

Hibernating grizzlies may sleep for three or four weeks without changing position. In most cases, though, the bears probably wake up fairly often. They rearrange their bedding and groom their fur. Then they fall back into slumber. But they do not fall into as deep a sleep as some animals do. A brown bear can be easily awakened, so they tend to choose dens far from possible disturbances.

The bears sleep until April or May. Depending upon the length of winter, a grizzly may sleep for as few as two and a half months to as many as seven.

Bears hibernate to survive. Winter cold and snow lessen the amount and variety of foods available, and make traveling difficult. A brown bear would use up more energy trying to find food than it would gain from the food it eventually found. Rather than take such a great risk, nature has ensured that the bear avoids the winter food problem altogether.

31

During January, grizzly cubs are born in the den. A mother normally has twins, but she may only have one cub or as many as four. At birth, a brown bear cub averages about 1 pound (.45 kg) in weight and measures about 1 foot (30 cm) in length. Each cub is covered with fine hair, and its eyes are closed. For three months, in the darkness of the female's den, the cubs fatten up on their mother's rich milk.

As the time of daylight lengthens and snowdrifts retreat, the grizzlies wake up—and stay awake. Scientists are not sure just how the brown bears receive their wake-up call. The bears may notice changes in whatever sunlight strays into their dens. More likely, they have a **biological clock**, or inner timing, that rouses them.

The first few days afield after hibernation are not likely to be easy for a hungry, drowsy brown bear. The grizzly may wander miles in search of a meal.

The bear's first spring dish may be carrion—perhaps a moose that starved to death or a seal that washed onto a beach. The first green shoots of spring appear soon, however, giving the bear a regular source of nutritious food. Meanwhile, its body systems return to normal.

Twin cubs, their first spring (left).

Females, of course, have a more difficult time finding food in the spring than the males do because they are slowed down by cubs. The cubs now weigh about 7 pounds (3.15 kg) each, and they need to **nurse** about every two hours.

Although a mother spends little time playing with her cubs, the cubs roughhouse with each other. Play is important. Through play, the cubs sharpen their reflexes and coordination. They wrestle and tumble, sniff, poke, and cuff. Meanwhile, mother is nearby for all the bear necessities of life—warmth, milk, and discipline with a growl, bite, or swat. By watching their mother, grizzly cubs quickly learn to sample solid foods and be alert for danger.

This cub has been sent up a tree by its mother.

The color of a cub's fur can change each year as it grows. A brown cub may become a blond adult.

A grizzly female is a patient, attentive mother. She will ferociously defend her cubs against anyone or anything that comes near. Despite the mother's care, grizzly cubs are sometimes killed by violent weather, a lack of healthy food, disease, male grizzlies, or, occasionally, wolf packs. No one knows how many cubs survive to adulthood, but it may be no more than half.

By their first autumn, the eight-month-old cubs still nurse, but they also gobble up more and more solid food—berries, nuts, roots, grasses, and meat. They are learning how to take and defend whatever they choose to eat. The cubs' mother does not catch a salmon or squirrel and divide it among her cubs. Driven by their own hunger, the grizzly cubs snatch bites of their mother's catch.

When the mother searches for a winter den, the cubs follow and sleep with her. The next spring and summer, they remain at her side, still nursing, hunting, and learning their way around their mother's home range.

The youngsters are nearly ready to live on their own when they leave the den for their third spring. Their mother begins to discourage nursing by making herself less available. Her milk starts to dry up. Usually the cubs are **weaned,** or separated from their mother's milk, before summer.

After weaning, the female's body prepares itself for another pregnancy. As the cubs run from the male who will be their mother's new mate, the bond between the cubs and their mother ends, normally forever. Now on their own, the cubs typically stay together for two or

The oldest wild grizzly on record lived to be 36. The average life span, however, is probably about half the record age. Grizzlies die naturally from old age, starvation, disease, or accidents. The only other threats to them come from people.

three years. They eventually set out to establish their own home ranges, many times on or near their mother's.

By the time it is six and a half years old, a grizzly is likely to mate and start a family of its own. With luck, a grizzly will live for many years and produce numerous litters of cubs.

Three hundred years ago, grizzlies lived across the West and Midwest. The great brown bear was considered a marvel of creation by many of the Native American nations who lived there. They feared its strength and respected its ability to survive winter without having to hunt. They felt a kinship with the humanlike bear, which sat on its rump, stood upright, snored, moaned, sighed, rotated its "arms," and shared their tastes in food. As a sign of respect for the bear, modern-day members of the Bear Clan of the Blackfeet nation will not say the name of the grizzly to people outside the clan.

The respect of Native Americans for the bear did not prevent many of them from killing grizzlies for the things they needed. They ate bear meat, used the fur and skin for clothing, and made jewelry with the claws.

Perhaps 10,000 brown bears lived in what is now California in 1800. California placed the grizzly on its official state seal, and the University of California chose "Golden Bears" for its teams' name. But California saved the grizzly only for its flags and official documents. The last wild grizzly in California was killed in 1924.

Real trouble for the grizzlies, though, did not begin until the dust of covered wagons and cattle herds began drifting over the American West in the 1800s. Grizzly habitats vanished, as more and more people settled in the area. Besides hunting grizzlies for their fur and meat, the settlers trapped, shot, and poisoned them because they thought the bears would attack their livestock and themselves. The brown bears vanished from the prairies and American West, remaining only in a few mountain strongholds, where they can still be found today.

41

In 1975, the United States Fish and Wildlife Service declared that grizzly bears in the lower 48 United States were **threatened.** That announcement made official what scientists had known for some time—the grizzly's future in these states is in doubt. The amount of habitat protected for them may not be enough to keep them from dying out, or becoming **extinct.**

In Alaska and Western Canada, much of the traditional grizzly country is still home to the brown bears. But the number of grizzlies will probably go down as more tourism, mining, oil drilling, and building go on in the Northwest. And as more people enter grizzly country for hiking, camping, rafting, and photographing, the chances of bears and people finding each other increases. Such meetings carry the chance of bringing death or injury to both people and bears. Whether or not anyone is seriously harmed, grizzlies that attack or act boldly toward people are moved to new areas or killed.

Despite its reputation, a grizzly is not a particularly vicious or unpredictable animal. Most brown bears are wary of people and avoid them. In fact, grizzlies often flee good bear habitat when it has been invaded by people and retreat to poor bear habitat, where dens and food are difficult to find. Under these tougher conditions, grizzlies may be more likely to attack when they meet people. In rare cases, the grizzlies may even eat parts of their victims. This happens because large predators naturally eat what they kill when they are hungry. But grizzlies don't normally view people as prey.

Grizzly-human encounters usually end peacefully. Larry Aumiller is a biologist who has studied the McNeil River brown bears—"McBears," he calls them—for more than 20 years. Each bear has an individual personality, he says. The problem is that a person who encounters a brown bear on a trail doesn't know that animal's personality. Nor does the bear know how the person will act.

Attacks on people usually occur for one of two reasons. Either a bear is startled by someone or a mother with cubs feels threatened. Most injuries caused by grizzlies could have been prevented if people had obeyed park rules or taken precautions suggested by wildlife managers.

In addition to grizzlies being killed for threatening people, brown bears are hunted in some parts of Alaska, Canada, and Montana. Sport hunting is carefully controlled, but each year a few hundred brown bears are killed by hunters. Grizzlies are also shot by people protecting their cattle and sheep.

Poachers, those who hunt animals illegally, kill brown bears every year as well. The body parts of the bears are then smuggled to Asian countries where some people believe certain bear parts, such as paws and gallbladders, have magical or disease-curing powers.

The future of North American brown bears does not depend so much on preventing poaching and controlling hunting, however, as on protecting the animals' habitat. If people want grizzlies to be anything more than animals found in a handful of parks and zoos, they will have to save **wilderness** habitats.

Wilderness is simply wild land left to itself—without highways, cities, farms, industries, buildings, and people. As most of the wilderness vanished in the Old West, so, too, did most of the grizzlies. By protecting wilderness areas in the West and Northwest, we protect a kingdom of peaks, glaciers, wild rivers, and mossy old forests. This is grizzly country, some of the most spectacular land on earth. And if we save it, we save the great brown bear itself.

GLOSSARY

biological clock: an inborn timing system responsible for various instinctive actions by an animal

carrion: rotting flesh of a dead animal

extinct: no longer living; when all members of a species have died

habitat: the specific kind of area where an animal naturally lives, such as a mountain meadow for a grizzly

hibernation: a sleeplike state in which an animal's body systems slow dramatically

home range: the territory in which a particular animal lives

homing instinct: an inborn ability to find the way back to one's home range after having been removed a long distance from it

migration: the act of moving seasonally from one location to another, usually for feeding or breeding

nurse: to suck the mother's milk

omnivore: an animal that eats both plant and animal material

poachers: people who hunt animals illegally

predator: an animal that hunts and kills other animals for food

prey: an animal that is hunted or taken for food by another animal

species: a scientific grouping of animals or plants that share similar characteristics, such as brown bears

subspecies: a group of members of a species that have specific physical differences from the rest of the species, such as Kodiak brown bears

threatened: species whose numbers have been reduced to the point that they may soon be in danger of extinction

wean: to force a cub to stop nursing

wilderness: a natural area of land that is basically undisturbed and not settled by people

INDEX

ABOUT THE AUTHOR

Lynn M. Stone is an author and photographer who has written more than 120 books for young readers about wildlife and natural history, including **Vultures,** also published by Carolrhoda Books. In addition to photographing wildlife, Mr. Stone enjoys fishing and traveling. A former teacher, he lives with his wife and daughter in Batavia, Illinois.